W9-BED-597

a book about girls, their bodies, and themselves

girl power

in the mirror

by Helen Cordes

CHAVEZ HIGH SCHOOL
LIBRARY
HOUSTON, TEXAS

Lerner Publications Company • Minneapolis

To Jesse and Zoe, two girls of power who are loved beyond description by their mother and father

Copyright © 2000 by Lerner Publications Company

All rights reserved. International copyright secured. No part of this book may be reproduced, stored in a retrieval system, or transmitted in any form or by any means—electronic, mechanical, photocopying, recording, or otherwise—without the prior written permission of Lerner Publications Company, except for the inclusion of brief quotations in an acknowledged review.

Lerner Publications Company
A Division of Lerner Publishing Group
241 First Avenue North
Minneapolis, MN 55401 U.S.A.

Website address: www.lernerbooks.com

The publisher thanks Shonagh Brent, who was photographed for the cover of this book.

Library of Congress Cataloging-in-Publication Data

Cordes, Helen, 1954–
    Girl power in the mirror: a book about girls, their bodies, and themselves / by Helen Cordes.
        p.   cm.
    Includes bibliographical references.
    Summary: Suggests ways for girls to develop self-esteem and become assertive in the face of pressures from advertisers, family, and peers to have a "perfect" body.
    ISBN 0-8225-2691-3 (lib. bdg. : alk. paper)
    1. Body image in adolescence—Juvenile literature. 2. Overweight women—Psychology—Juvenile literature. 3. Obesity—Psychological aspects—Juvenile literature. 4. Self-acceptance in adolescence—literature. [1. Self-esteem. 2. Assertiveness (Psychology) 3. Weight control.] I. Title.
BF724.3.B55C67   2000
306.4—dc21   97–1085

Manufactured in the United States of America
1 2 3 4 5 6 – JR – 05 04 03 02 01 00

Contents

chapter one

A Rainbow of Girls

I'm not as developed as I hope to become, but I'm satisfied. As far as being pretty, I'm definitely not going to become the next Cindy Crawford, but it's all good.

— Meki, 14

Ready for a game show? It stars you, and it's called "Meet the Mirror!" The rules are simple. Just find a mirror (good lighting, please). Then ask yourself: Are you pretty? Be thorough—rate everything from hair to face to skin to clothes to shoes.

How'd you do? If you're like lots of girls, you rated yourself . . . not so hot. Surveys—such as a poll done by the American Association of University Women (AAUW) of 3,000 fourth to tenth graders—revealed that most girls can't look in a mirror and say, "I'm pretty!" or even "I'm okay!"

Ready for round two? The question this time: Do you have a nice size and shape? Check out everything again—from height to weight to muscles to curves.

Did your score go up? If not, join the ranks again. Lots of girls are dissatisfied with their body shape and size. In one recent study of preteen and teen girls in San Francisco, 80 percent of girls as young as nine years old were dieting.

Probably everybody—girls and boys, kids and adults—thinks at least occasionally about how they look. And probably most people have changed the way they look at one time or another to look "better." They're following a natural human urge that goes back to cave people, who drew colorful designs on their bodies or put their hair into "boney-tails."

Many girls think more than ever about their looks as they head into their teen years. It's no wonder—there's a lot going on with your body during these years. There are emerging curves, hair that sprouts in places that aren't your head, and, sooner or later, menstruation. With menstruation come some Big Body Questions about

I do not like my face and body size. I don't like anything about myself.

—Sasha, 12

things like sex and pregnancy. Of course, a girl is going to notice her body more than ever.

But some people worry that girls care too much about the way they look. Sasha, 12, is one of many real girls you'll hear from in this book. She doesn't like what she sees in her mirror. "I don't like my face and body size," she says. "I don't like anything about myself." Boys seem to care a lot less about their weight and their looks. In one survey of 8,000 fifth to ninth graders, 60 percent of the boys said they were just fine with how they looked. Another study of 3,000 Vermont teens found lots of boys wanted to put on a few pounds, not diet!

Like a Girl

Why the difference between girls and boys? The difference probably goes back to the day a person is born a certain sex—either female or male. Right away, many people treat a baby "like a girl" or "like a boy." Studies show that girl babies get compliments for their looks. Boy babies get praise for what they do. This pattern is based on what's called a gender expectation. The pattern continues as kids get older. You might notice the pattern at home and at school.

Many people say this pattern can also be a gender bias. A gender bias is a gender expectation that turns out to be damaging. For example, advertisers selling things like make-up, hair products, and clothes show mostly one version of a girl: pretty, tall, and thin. Some girls end up thinking they're expected to look that way.

This expectation may be damaging, some people say. When girls believe they're not thin enough, goes the argument, too many go on unhealthy diets or exercise programs. In extreme cases, these can result in illness or even death. Girls who feel they fall short of the ideal may start blaming themselves and doubting their potential to do *anything* very well.

> *M*y thighs were too big, I was unshapely, and there was nothing distinct about me.
>
> —Reanna, 14

Other people disagree that the emphasis on looks is harmful to girls. Putting a lot of effort into your looks won't hurt you, they say. In fact, it gets rewards. Lindsay, 11, says thin, pretty girls are usually "popular, look cool, and have a cool boyfriend."

Lindsay could be right. When researchers do experiments with women, they often find pretty women get more attention than less attractive women do. In one experiment, an attractive woman and a less attractive woman pretended their cars had broken down on a highway. The more attractive woman got more offers for help.

Alyssa, 14, remembers seeing a similar experiment on the TV show *20/20*. The producers filmed a woman in a bar. The woman was dressed to look unattractive. A man sitting near her ignored her. Then the woman left and returned. This time, she wore attractive makeup and clothes. The man near her was suddenly interested and tried to get her attention. "That's the reality," says Alyssa. "Being attractive has benefits—lots and lots of them." Besides, it's not that easy to just "not care," adds Sasha, the girl who didn't like anything about herself.

> Some people tell me not to worry about the way I look. That just makes me feel worse.
>
> —Sasha, 12

What do you think? Are some girls treated differently from other girls according to their looks and size? If there's a difference, is it bad, or good, or a mix?

In this book, we'll examine all the different ways girls' looks and body shapes affect what they think about themselves and how they are treated. We'll see how their looks affect what they do. We'll take a peek at different times and places and the ways girls wanted to look. There will be some surprises here!

All along, we'll hear from lots of girls themselves and from people who care about girls. They'll be

The Truth about the
Hot New Look

Ever notice how the "hot new look" changes all the time? One year, the look might be loose clothes and makeup in pale shades. The next year, the look includes close-cut clothes and makeup in bold colors.

The makers of clothes and beauty products want fashion trends to keep changing. That way, we'll buy their new products (and they'll make money). If we kept being happy with the clothes and makeup we had, we wouldn't buy stuff nearly as often, right? The clothing and beauty industries bank on us being fashion slaves. Too often, they're right on target.

talking about ways girls can learn to love and respect their own bodies. After all, the person who tells you the most about how you should look is likely to be . . . you! We'll see how a rainbow of girls are learning and growing with spirit.

chapter two

The Fat Problem

When I put on an outfit, I always
wonder if I look fat in it.

—Julie, 14

Does Julie's comment sound familiar? Bet you've
heard—maybe said or thought—something like
this, which makes you totally normal. Surveys
show that most girls sometimes talk about disliking
their body size, and some girls talk about it a lot.

And why shouldn't they? Everywhere girls look,
they see messages that tell them thinner is better.
Open a magazine—there are thin, thin models
everywhere. Usually they're wearing fabulous
clothes and being adored by megacute guys. In
between the fashion articles, there are likely to be
articles on dieting and exercise. Turn on a music

video or watch a movie. You see more thin women with—you guessed it—fab clothes and cute guys. Billboards—ditto.

Feel hungry? You've got to eat low fat, goes the message, and watch those calories. Want to go for a walk? You might pass that diet center, health club, or exercise studio near you. Americans spend thirty-three billion dollars a year at these places and on diet products, trying to lose weight.

> *I hate not being able to think about how anything tastes while I eat out, because others are thinking, "My God, she is too fat to eat that way. She should feel guilty."*
>
> —Becca, 14

The Weight Mystery

No one would likely choose to be a lot overweight and endure the cruel teasing that sometimes happens. But here's something that might surprise you: most girls who say they are overweight have a perfectly normal weight! All the girls in one study (by the Melpomene Institute, a research center in Minnesota) weighed amounts appropriate for their frames. Yet three-fourths of them said they were too fat or they needed to watch their weight. Many other studies have produced similar results.

Health researchers agree that our natural size is the result of the genes we inherit from our parents. Our genes determine the number of fat cells in our bodies. Our genes also determine our metabolic rates. Metabolism refers to the process by which food is changed into energy, waste products, weight, and new cells. Different people have different rates of metabolism. That's why some people can eat a lot and never gain weight, while others gain weight even when they don't eat much. Given the genes we inherit, guess how many of us will naturally have the tall, thin bodies models have? Fewer than 5 percent.

Yes, eating healthy foods and exercising moderately can help keep your body at its natural size. But there's not much you can do to change what your natural size is. Becoming model thin is impossible for most of us.

The average American woman is five feet four and weighs 135 pounds. Yet too often, girls don't compare themselves to women in everyday life. "Some of my friends want to go on diets when they already have a skinny body," notes Pauline, 15. The reason? "They compare each other to models."

> Some of my friends want to go on a diet when they already have a skinny body.
>
> —Pauline, 15

If you take a close look at the media (TV, movies, magazines, and the like), you may agree. The media's view of the ideal body size for young women seems to be about five feet nine, 110 pounds. But would you be willing to do what a model does to stay at her weight? While a few models insist that they don't diet or exercise much, most models spend two to three hours a day exercising. They rarely eat more than skimpy portions of low-fat food and constantly worry about their weight.

One Example

Esquire magazine put actress Michelle Pfeiffer on its cover, with a headline saying that "What Michelle Pfeiffer Needs Is . . . Absolutely Nothing." Turns out that Pfeiffer did need something—several thousand dollars worth of makeup work and photo fixups that trimmed her chin, took out facial lines, and made other improvements!

Models are also made to look better than they naturally would. Plastic surgery, expensive clothes, and makeup applied by experts all enhance their natural looks. Models also get help from computer and airbrush techniques that can alter photos. These techniques can make them appear thinner or more curvaceous or prettier than they really are.

Here's something else to consider. A relatively small number of people produce or work in the media. Because the media is all around us, the opinion of this small group is all around us, too. We seem to see their ideal—that five-feet-nine, 110-pound body—everywhere. But for lots of people, that notion of what is ideal is way off.

Image vs. Self-Image

Many African Americans, for example, think that some pounds, particularly on the hips and thighs, look great! That fact makes it easier for many African-American girls to accept their bodies. A University of Arizona survey of teenagers showed that 90 percent of white girls were *not* happy with their weight and size, but 70 percent of the African-American girls *were* happy!

In many cultures around the world, particularly those in which many people go hungry, a plump person is one who is fortunate to have enough to eat. In Jamaica, a person who has more weight is often thought to have more happiness. According to author Elisa Sobo, Jamaicans get concerned when a friend loses her "sweet fat." The friend's weight loss is a sign that she is unhappy. In many other parts of the world, the women considered most desirable are those Americans would call "fat."

Even in the United States, the superthin look has not always been the most desir- able. Your library may have issues of fashion magazines from the 1950s and 1960s. Flip through a few and see how much bigger the women in ads and photos were back then. They look average! In fact, mod- els in the 1960s weighed just a bit (one-fifteenth) less than the average woman. In the late 1990s, models weigh much less (nearly one-fourth less!) than the average woman.

"I really don't think the way most girls look in magazines is a realistic way to look," says Evelyn, 14. "But I'll tell you the truth. When I see models or people on TV, I say to myself, 'Oh, I wish I looked like that.'"

What happens to girls when they can't stop wishing and trying for the "ideal" figure? When girls look in the mirror and continue to see a body

> *Looks are pretty unimportant when you step out of magazine and TV land.*
>
> —Reanna, 14

they don't like, they develop a poor "body image." Researchers Deborah Tolman and Elizabeth Debold estimate that two-thirds of young girls have a distorted body image.

This can lead girls to lots of self-destructive behavior, say Tolman, Debold, and many other experts. Many normal-sized girls, and even thin girls, diet and exercise continually. Hundreds of thousands of girls develop eating disorders such as anorexia (starving themselves) or bulimia (eating a lot and then purging the food by throwing up or using laxatives). These disorders can harm a girl's health or even kill her.

For lots of girls, having a poor body image means losing confidence about other parts of their lives. Often girls who believe their bodies don't look good enough avoid drawing attention to themselves. They might not speak up in class. They might avoid participating in sports, school plays, or clubs. They might even accept bad behavior. Franzlyne, 14, considers herself "too fat and not that pretty." She says, "If I don't feel good about how I look, I don't stand up for myself." Worst of all, when a girl gets preoccupied with losing weight, she has lots less attention to give to the rest of her life.

So what can a girl do to keep her body image sensible, strong, and healthy? Here are some strategies.

Notice *Your Feelings*

When you feel as though you need to shrink your body or that you need to stuff yourself with food, think about what emotions you are feeling at the time. When girls are truthful with themselves, they acknowledge that sometimes things like starting a strict diet or exercise program or wolfing down a carton of ice cream happen during times of stress.

For example, fourteen-year-old Yong says she sometimes feels humiliated by classmates who call her hurtful names, such as "Chink" and "fat-ass." Her response is to overeat. After a group of friends rejected Yong during a summer program, she quit and "sat home over the summer eating."

I f I don't feel good about how I look, I don't stand up for myself.

—Franzlyne, 14

Other girls say that unhealthy eating or dieting behavior happens when they feel lonely, angry, or "not good enough." Jessica, 15, starved herself because she believed she was "worthless" unless she was thin. Happily, she found help. Some feel that they would be more accepted by classmates or parents if they were thinner.

Some research, such as a survey of 36,000 Minnesota teens, has found that girls with eating disorders are more likely than other girls to be dealing with big problems such as sexual abuse (unwanted sexual touching by someone) or family problems (such as having a parent who drinks too much).

Sometimes the stresses girls face leave them feeling they are not in control of their lives. People who help girls with body image problems and eating disorders say that girls try to gain a sense of control by controlling their weight and food intake. But they often ask girls: Are you *really* gaining control or are your behaviors gaining control over you?

Write Down
Your Feelings

Whenever you look in a mirror and see yourself as "fat" or whenever you think you are eating unusually, stop for a moment. Think about how you're feeling. Get a notebook or diary and write down your feelings. If you come up with a problem or emotion that's bothering you, think about whether eating or dieting will help with the problem.

I worry so much about how I look.

—Barri Ann, 11

Don't feel bad if you go ahead with the behavior anyway. Just stick with the writing process for a while—maybe for a week or a month. Writing in your diary may help you think of different ways to tackle some problems. It may just help you understand more about yourself.

Compare Yourself to Real Girls

Take a look—maybe in gym class or at the swimming pool—at what other girls' bodies *really* look like. That's what Reanna did. Sure, a few girls' bodies may look almost "perfect." But most bodies don't.

Bodies come in an amazing variety of shapes and different-sized body parts. If so many girls aren't "perfect," then doesn't it seem that the idea of perfect may be kind of ridiculous?

As you make comparisons, be sure to look at the bodies of girls whom you like and respect—your friends or girls who are so nice and interesting that you'd like to become friends. Chances are, they don't have perfect bodies. Yet people—people like you!—want to be around them.

> My best friend likes me for who I am.
>
> —Liz, 16

People Who Radiate

A few years ago I thought I was pretty plain. My thighs were too big, I was unshapely, and there was nothing distinct about me. I made a point of looking at all kinds of women and seeing that my thighs were normal and that I am quite striking and distinct when I want to be.

Looks are pretty unimportant when you step out of magazine and TV land. Looks don't change friendships or how much people like you. I'm attracted to people who radiate, regardless of looks. It's always personality, vitality, and style that grab me.

—*Reanna, 14*

Take a Break *from Unreality*

Consider taking an occasional vacation from looking at fashion magazines. An Arizona State University study asked young women about their

CHAVEZ HIGH SCHOOL
LIBRARY
HOUSTON, TEXAS

body images. (Again, all the young women in the study were of normal size.) The study found that the young women who frequently looked at fashion magazines were much more likely to be dissatisfied with their bodies than those who looked at the magazines less often. The fans of the fashion magazines were also more likely to have eating disorders.

When you do look at pictures of models and actresses, ask yourself: Is this the way most girls and women look? Or check out the women who are pictured in the media because of their accomplishments. You'll find a broad range of looks among women who are happy and successful.

Make Friends with Food

A lot of girls start developing some strange opinions about food as they move into their teens. Certain foods—maybe most foods—start to seem "bad." These girls try to avoid those foods because the foods might cause a weight gain.

Other girls are scared that certain foods will cause out-of-control behavior. You've surely heard this one: "If I have one cookie, then I'll want to eat the whole package!"

Still other girls worry that people will judge them by what they eat. "Like if you eat one potato chip, people will think you're a pig," notes Jessica, 14.

The Food Game

Here's a game to reacquaint yourself with the joys of food. Ask a friend or a group of friends to collect samples of several kinds of yummy treats without telling you what they are. Then put on a blindfold and have a friend hand you the treats one by one.

Try to guess what each treat is. As you taste the treats, focus on the delicious qualities of each. Figure out what you like about the taste—the sweetness, the bite, the texture, or whatever. Famous winemakers and gourmet chefs use this technique—closing their eyes and savoring tiny samples—to create fine wines and new recipes.

After the game, try to notice and enjoy all the different foods you eat. Chances are, if you make a point of really enjoying the first serving, you probably won't want to eat several more.

Lots of girls can't see food for what it is—the fuel that is needed to make your body and mind work their best. That's why it's important to choose healthy foods most of the time. Eating is also a pleasure that's even more fun when shared with friends. Why deny yourself that?

As for dealing with people who might criticize what you eat in public, well, forget it. There will always be some people who think that girls should be skinnier than they are. Ask yourself if pleasing them is more important than pleasing yourself?

Ask for Help

If you are doing unhealthy things to change your body, please talk to someone you trust, such as a friend, a parent, or a school counselor. Be sure to find someone who can help you get help. If you can't decide whether your behavior is unhealthy or not, talk to someone who can help you decide.

Remember that eating disorders are a serious problem. Usually girls who have anorexia start losing their ability to see that they are losing dangerous amounts of weight. Because of their poor body image, they believe that they are still "fat" even when the mirror shows that they are extremely thin.

When girls stop eating enough, some of them die of starvation-related health problems. Bulimia can cause many problems with important parts of the body, such as the heart, the kidneys, the stomach, and the liver. Repeated vomiting can also cause rotting teeth and throat problems.

Make Friends with You

How much do you like you? If you don't like your body, it's hard to feel that you love, or even like, you. Yet if you don't love yourself at least some of the time, then how will others love you and want to be around you?

The need to be loved is powerful. Author Terry Nicholetti Garrison talks about that need in her book *Fed Up! A Woman's Guide to Freedom from the Diet/ Weight Prison.* Terry asked high school girls why they wanted to be thinner or prettier. "All the answers boil down to 'I want someone to love me,'" she explains. Terry then points out the love success (not!) of some of America's thinnest and prettiest people— movie stars and models. "Look at their high break-up rate and the things they do to keep their shape," Terry notes.

I have big feet and freckles, and I can't change those things, so why worry about it.

—Rachel, 18

Terry is an advocate for "size acceptance." People should accept and appreciate their bodies no matter what the size, she urges.

Most people who speak out about size acceptance are self-described "fat" people. They argue that heavy people should not be treated unkindly or discriminated against. They point to much evidence showing that heavy people are often physically fit and normal eaters as well.

Laura Fraser is five feet, six inches tall and weighs 155 pounds. In her book *Losing It,* she says medical authorities agreed that her size was healthy and normal. Since Fraser eats well and exercises moderately, her size—considered "overweight" in our culture—is simply a result of her genes.

You don't have to be fat or overweight to practice size acceptance. You simply have to remind yourself that your body is *you!* And why would you want to dislike you? When you accept—maybe even *like*—your body, then you can focus more on all the other wonderful things you have going for you.

Many girls aren't always happy with how they look, but they've found ways to keep that unhappiness from taking over their lives. Julie knows that when she's worried about how she looks, "I don't

> *Looks don't change friendships or how much people like you.*
>
> —Reanna, 14

have fun, and I am not comfortable because it is on my mind." She starts reminding herself of exciting things going on in her life—things that have nothing to do with her looks.

Barri Ann, 11, worries "so much about how I look." She tries doing something fun to get her mind off her looks. She says, "I read, listen to music, watch TV, talk to a friend, go outside and have some fun, or just hang out."

Becca, 14, admits she'd love to look like the women she sees in magazines. But she reminds herself that even models have flaws that are airbrushed out of photos. Becca questions whether being thin and pretty will really put girls ahead in the world. Getting what you want out of life doesn't come from looks, she believes, but from "pushing yourself." She says, "You are what you make of what God gave you, and that is all that can be asked."

chapter three

Liking Your Looks
(Really!)

I hate what I look like. It makes me feel horrible.

—*Barri Ann*, 11

$\mathscr{R}$emember our game show, "Meet the Mirror!" and the surveys in which girls rated themselves low on looks, while boys were generally much more satisfied with their looks? Well, why does it matter that lots of girls think they're not very pretty?

Girls themselves admit that when they're not confident about their looks, they're not very confident about other things in their lives. "I get worried sometimes that I'm not good enough for someone because of my looks," says Becky, 15.

When people aren't happy about their abilities and worth, they have "low self-esteem." Boys generally have higher self-esteem than girls do. An AAUW survey of high school students found half the boys were happy with themselves. But the girls? Fewer than a third were happy with themselves. Self-esteem seems to drop as girls enter junior high or high school, the survey concluded.

But wait a minute! Are girls going to stand for guys showing them up on the self-esteem score? Raising your self-esteem isn't necessarily easy, but it can be done. Self-esteem is not a set thing. Like your physical health, the health of your self-esteem can be good at some times and poor at others.

Judge *Everything*

Having a healthy self-esteem involves looking at *everything* about yourself—including the good things about your personality, your talents, and your life. Then give yourself some credit for your assets.

Of course, your self-esteem is partly affected by how good you think you look. No one is suggesting that you try to forget your looks. But there are also ways to change your personal

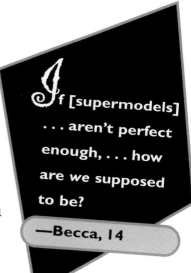

If [supermodels] . . . aren't perfect enough, . . . how are we supposed to be?

—Becca, 14

prettiness ratings. And they don't involve plastic surgery!

The first step is to look at what you compare yourself to. "I am like most girls in that I turn to magazines and television to compare myself," says Becca. She knows that many pictures of models can be unrealistic "fakes." Becca asks, "If [supermodels] all have flaws they must cover up artificially . . . if they aren't perfect enough . . . how are *we* supposed to be?"

Comparing your prettiness to that of models is guaranteed to create massive insecurity. And it just doesn't make sense. For starters, there are very few girls who have the features required for modeling. And as we noted earlier, models get lots of unnatural help to achieve their "natural" prettiness.

Lots of girls and women are angry that magazines, TV, and movies don't show more average-looking women. Their protests have had some effect. In the past few years, several fashion magazines have occasionally used nonmodels in fashion spreads. Some clothing catalogs feature not-so-perfect models.

Reality Check

But don't expect to see a lot of this. Advertisers selling stuff to make us "prettier" (hair, makeup, and skin-care products) are spending lots of money to convince us to buy their goods. Girls and women spend twenty billion dollars each year on these products. We would not likely spend so much money if we didn't have the hope that the products would make us more beautiful. That hope is fueled by the beautiful (but not realistic) models we see.

The same goes for clothing. Clothing companies will mostly keep showing their clothes on tall, thin, beautiful models. The clothes look most enticing, they think, on that kind of woman. Girls and women will then more likely buy the clothes—along with the dream that they will look like the models in the clothes.

So what's the solution? Should we refuse to look at fashion magazines, advertising, music videos, movies, and billboards? That would be pretty tough. Billboards alone would be hard to avoid. A better option is for girls to simply use their own reality test when they look at women in the media.

Let's give it a try. Okay, we're looking at a magazine photo with a five-feet-nine, 110-pound girl.

I wish I could look like a supermodel, but magazines [don't show] the way most people look.

—Andrea, 14

She has beautiful skin, hair, and clothes. She's smiling, snuggling up against a buff guy who gazes at her in adoration. It's easy to imagine that the two are in a blissful, romantic relationship.

Hello! It's likely the two models don't even know one another. They probably had never met before the photo shoot. They're being paid to look like they're crazy about each other.

Before the picture was taken, a small army of people spent many hours and lots of money on the hair, face, and skin of these models. The photographer took lots of pictures. The photo that was most flattering to the models was chosen. It's likely, too, that the chosen photo was altered in some way to make her, or both of them, look still better. What's real here? *Nada!*

Truer Standards

Let's agree that our current beauty standards are way out of whack, but let's also look at some different standards we could have. Remember how we learned that African-American girls are more likely to be happy with their looks? That's mostly because they compare themselves to other African-American girls and women—not to models.

White girls told researchers Sheila Parker and Mimi Nichter that the ideal girl was someone who

When I look at the television, I see images of women too beautiful to touch. These women are delicate and feminine and don't seem to have a care in the world.

At the other end of the spectrum, I see the women of my own culture, the women I grew up with. I admire these tough, determined women, many of whom are single parents and sole providers, for keeping themselves and their families together.

This woman does not look dainty or feminine but has the signs of hard work and worry etched on her face. I don't admire her pain but rather the living proof that she has made it through hardship.

—Gabrielle, 19
excerpted from YO!

looked . . . well, pretty much like a Barbie doll. African-American girls gave this description of the ideal girl—she has a good head on her shoulders, has a nice personality, and gets along well with other people.

Doesn't this sound like a better standard for comparison? Take a look around at your class-mates and think about the ones who seem to know where they're going, the ones who are truly happy. They're not model material, right?

It is true that often the prettiest girls seem to have the best deal—attention from boys, maybe more people who want to be around them. But are you sure they're the happiest ones? Or that they have confidence in other parts of their lives? Here's what was discovered in one of several studies that have looked at whether attractive people are happier. They're not, a Univer-sity of Illinois study found. In fact, attractive people often expect more because of their looks—like three date offers for Saturday night instead of one or none. When the attrac-tive people in the study didn't get special treatment, they were disappointed.

As for the guy factor, let's be honest—if a guy

> If [looks are] all a guy is looking for, then they probably don't care about what's inside.
>
> —Amy, 14

is only interested in your looks and in nothing else, is he the kind of guy you'd want anyway? "If a guy is going to like a girl, it should be for her personality," says Briar, 14.

Remember, too, that guys aren't the only ones who prize attractiveness. Girls often pick the cutest guys—not the nicest or most talented—for their "most wanted" list. If girls don't want guys to be shallow about looks, girls can't be shallow either.

Dr. Anne Kearny-Cooke, a psychologist who works with teens, has found that some guys say they value things like confidence, smarts, and a sense of humor in girls more than they value looks. (Where *are* those guys, anyway?)

Whether or not confidence is something most guys like, confidence is a reflection of your "inner beauty." It means that you appreciate and enjoy your unique talents and personality. Confidence can make a big difference. "When I feel good about myself from the inside, looks stop being so important," says Reanna, 14.

Outer and *Inner Beauty*

Discovering your inner beauty doesn't mean you forget about outer beauty. In fact, girls who've become confident say they now have more fun with things like hair styling, makeup, and clothes.

They feel more free to create their own unique look when they want to, instead of rushing to buy the latest styles or struggling to look exactly like their friends.

Here's how Carolyn, 14, gets her own look. "I usually get my styles from the basement, digging through my parents' old clothes," she says. "I like people to look at me and say, 'Look at that *freak!*' Not that I want to look ugly—just different."

Erin, 13, is on her way to developing her own style. "Sometimes, if I'm wearing something that I think is really cute, my friends will think I'm strange, and then I'll change into something else. I think I have to learn to be my own person and wear what I like to wear."

Looking the way you want tells the world that you know who you are, and that you're happy with yourself. That was the philosophy behind a "feminist fashion show" held at Seattle Central Community College. "We had models of all different shapes, sizes, and colors," says Melyssa Rice, who helped organize the show and modeled in it. "They each chose their own look, and then spoke about why they picked it after they modeled it."

I get depressed after looking at [pictures of supermodels], but if I'm with normal people I feel great.

—Andrea, 14

As a teen, Rice was obsessed with her looks. "Appearance could make or break a day," she remembers. Now, she says, "I'll dress according to my mood. I feel like I'm reclaiming fashion for myself."

You might want to put on your own "unfashion fashion show" with your friends. Or maybe you could have a "truth session" with a friend or friends you trust, with each girl telling the truth about how she thinks she looks. The chances are very high that your friends have similar insecurities about how they look.

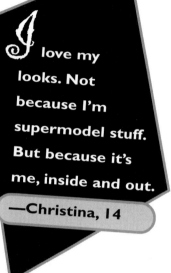

I love my looks. Not because I'm supermodel stuff. But because it's me, inside and out.

—Christina, 14

Talk It *Out*

Talking together, you and your friends may be able to build confidence by pointing out each other's talents and special traits. You might even find that your friends think you're prettier than you think you are. "Most of the time, when you think you look bad, you really don't from another person's point of view," says Erica, 14.

Talking honestly about looks will also help if one of you is being teased because of her looks.

Classmates teased Tiffany, 12. They called Tiffany skinny and nerdy. She wrote to *New Moon,* a magazine written for and by girls, and got some long-distance advice through their "Ask a Girl" column. Girls like Casey, 13, answered Tiffany in the column. Casey said she'd been teased for her looks, too. She said the teasing stopped when she stopped reacting to it.

Tiffany tried Casey's approach and liked it. "I learned that ignoring things like that is the best," wrote Tiffany. Other girls noted in *New Moon* that teasing usually comes from people who feel insecure about themselves. These people tease others to make themselves feel better.

Don't forget to take the long-range view when you're having one of those "I can't believe I look like this" days. Allie, 15, has those days. "I do find myself worrying about what I look like," says Allie. "But I know that later on, people aren't going to remember that bad hair day or the day my socks didn't match; they're going to remember me for who I am. As I watch other people at school, I see that they all have a bad hair day every once in a while.

> *Most of the time, when you think you look bad, you really don't from another person's point of view.*
>
> —Erica, 14

So I've learned that your true friends like you for who you are, not what you look like."

Pauline, 15, also looks down the road. "To stop worrying about how I look, I start to think about what's inside me. My intelligence is going to last longer than my looks, and will take me farther in this world."

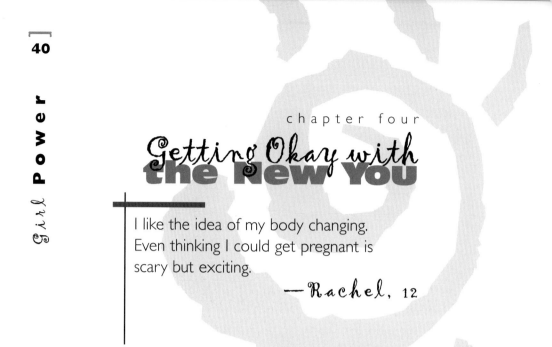

chapter four

Getting Okay with the New You

I like the idea of my body changing. Even thinking I could get pregnant is scary but exciting.

—*Rachel*, 12

*H*ow are you feeling about the Big Body Business that's been going on with you or is coming up for you real soon? You know—all the stuff like getting breasts, hips, and periods. Stuff like mood swings, acne attacks, and doing (or not doing) sexual things.

Growing up can be a complicated business, leaving girls feeling happy and worried at the same time. For example, practically all girls look forward to getting some curves in the "right" places. "I can't wait until I get a bigger chest," declares Desiree Ann, 11, "'cause I'll feel much more like a woman than a little girl."

But while girls are usually ecstatic when their breasts bloom, many aren't so thrilled about growing hips as well. "I know that it's just because I'm maturing, but it makes me feel fat!" complains Jenny, 11.

Many girls are also eager to begin close encounters of the romantic kind. But they can find the decisions they need to make difficult as well as complicated. "Everybody at my school is always talking about sex," says Laurie, 15. "I couldn't wait to be part of that. I think that's a lot of why I first had sex. But now I feel like I got into sex too deep, too soon."

There's no denying that the teen years are particularly tricky. The changes they bring can also be exciting and wonderful. Lots of girls are finding great ways to figure out—and then enjoy!—their teen years. Their advice seems to boil down to three basic guidelines.

When I feel good about myself from the inside, looks stop being so important.

—Reanna, 14

Listening to Your Body

Many girls and women notice that before their period comes, their emotions change. They might be more outspoken or more defensive than usual. But women, like Tamara Slayton, who have studied the menstrual cycle say that many women simply desire being alone or quiet during this time.

Of course, not every girl or woman has mood changes connected with her period. Whether or not your mood changes isn't important—either way is normal. But you could try paying attention to whether you feel differently at different cycle times. The more you are aware of your feelings, the more you'll know about yourself.

1. Get the Facts

Whether you're curious about what menstruation actually feels like or worried about how to make the best choices about getting intimate with someone, the answers are out there. Remember, every woman you know has gone through the same process of growing up. That's why you shouldn't feel shy about asking questions of someone you trust, such as your mom, a school counselor, or an older friend. If you're comfortable with your dad, try him. Okay, he probably won't deliver on "how menstruation feels," but he is a former teenage guy, and he might have some good advice.

There are also a lot of good books and articles about everything from periods to pregnancy. And there are organizations that can help.

2. Decide *How You Feel*

After you get the info you need, try to decide how you—not everybody else—feel about things. Lots of girls want their first periods to be private; others tell all their friends. Your feelings, whatever they are, are valid.

Here's one example of why it's important to figure things out for yourself. Remember how Laurie started having sex too soon partly because everybody else said they were? "It turns out

> *E*verybody at my school is always talking about sex.
>
> —Laurie, 15

that only two or three people were really doing it. Everyone else was just talking like they were," she recalls.

When people feel they are expected to behave like others around them, that's called "peer pressure." If a girl can figure out what she wants—not what she thinks she should want because of peer pressure—she can make a decision that is "true" for her.

3. Act on *Your Feelings*

After you figure out how you feel, try to act on your feelings. Sometimes it may be hard to do things the way you've decided is right for you, especially if it's not what others seem to be doing. But you will feel proud of yourself if you follow your own heart. And soon you will know that your decision was the right one.

Consider joining with other girls who are going through the same changes you are. In many cities, the YWCA has a "Girls Club" that meets after school. In the club, girls can discuss how to make good decisions about things like health and sexuality. In another YWCA program, PACT, teens are learning decision-making skills so that they can help other teens. The Girl Scouts also has programs that focus on health and sexuality. So does Girls, Incorporated.

Guideline #1

Let's get specific about how these three guidelines work and can be applied to real life. We'll start with the way your body is changing—or not changing—as you grow older.

Many girls get worried that they're not developing at the "right" time. Maybe they haven't started their periods yet or their breasts are not developing. They get bummed about cramps when their period starts or about getting lopsided breasts. They wonder whether there's an end to acne invasions and confusing moods. "It's strange," says Sasha, 12. "One day I can be as happy as anyone can be. Then the next day I can be really unhappy."

Here comes guideline #1: Get the facts. Health experts agree that just about all of the above is normal. Moodiness and acne are a result of the same hormones that create your more-welcomed body changes.

As for the timing of all these changes, it varies widely. To prove this, just scope out other girls' bodies at the pool and see how girls of the same age can be at all different stages. One girl may be very young when she starts developing. Another may be many years older. Any one girl will be behind or ahead of her friends at any given time. If you're still concerned, consider having a doctor's checkup.

Guideline #2

I know [the change] is just because I'm maturing, but it makes me feel fat.

—Jenny, 11

Of course, even if you reassure yourself that you're normal, you still may not feel great about your changing body. Here's where you use guideline #2: Decide how you feel. Girls can make a decision to simply spend less time wishing their bodies looked or acted differently. Becky, 15, saw a lot of changes in herself and her friends in just a couple of years. She advised her friends not to worry: "We'll all catch up one day," she says.

Some girls go even farther. They not only accept the fact that the changes in their bodies are okay but also celebrate those changes. Some girls are beginning to celebrate their first period as an important signpost to becoming a woman. To mark the occasion, they have a party with their friends. Another way to celebrate is dinner out with just your mom or family. That's what Jessica did the day she got her first period.

These girls are courageous, because they are making their own way against some powerful peer pressure. In our culture, menstruation seems to be considered an embarrassing thing. Even girls like Jessica who are happy to get their period get shy about telling others about it. "I used to think that

Changes to *Celebrate*

After four years of waiting for my period and lying to a few friends, it had finally come!! I was so happy. Walking down the hall back to class, I felt so wonderful. I was totally strutting my stuff.

When I got home from school, I told my mom. She was very happy and got a little mushy, but it wasn't too bad. That night, we went out to eat, and I got to pick the restaurant. Also, my parents bought me a CD!

—Jessica, 14

when I got my period, I'd never be able to tell my mom," she recalls.

Often girls say they're embarrassed to be seen buying menstrual products like pads or tampons. Did you know that, until a few years ago, manufacturers of menstrual products weren't allowed to advertise them on TV? Advertising menstrual products was thought to be in "bad taste."

Shame about menstruation goes back hundreds of years in many cultures. Menstruating females were considered bad luck in some cultures, say sociologists Karen Ericksen Paige and Jeffery Paige. In quite a few societies, menstruating women were forbidden to appear in public.

Scholars such as the Paiges who study menstruation believe the reason was that men in these cultures were afraid of women's power. Women were the only ones who could have babies. Menstruation made that power obvious every month. Rules like the one saying menstruating women must hide were meant to lessen women's power.

When girls say "no" to shame and embarrassment over body processes like menstruation, they are also saying "yes" to liking—maybe even loving!—their bodies. "Loving your body" may sound like a weird concept, but it can go a long way toward making you feel good about yourself during these years of change.

Sex and Guideline #2

When girls listen to their bodies and emotions, they are much more able to enjoy the changes and challenges of their teen years. This self-knowledge is particularly helpful when girls are dealing with stuff like dating and sexual activity.

Just as girls first experience body changes such as menstruation at different ages, girls also develop an interest in romance and feelings of sexual attraction at different ages. You may be eleven or whatever and not have much interest in romance at all. Or you may be fifteen or whatever and have lots of interest.

Either way, your feelings are okay. Different feelings can happen at different times, or at the same time. You might begin to have some mushy thoughts about someone and then find yourself experiencing sexual feelings, too. You'll know if you notice a tingly or warm feeling in your genitals or breasts when you think about sexual activities like kissing or touching. All humans have sexual feelings. These feelings get stronger as we mature.

Girls may also experience romantic or sexual feelings that are not "heterosexual" (heterosexual people are attracted to people of the opposite sex). These feelings, which may occur once or occasionally, just happen to some people. It does not necessarily mean that you are a "lesbian" (a female who is attracted to females) or "bisexual" (someone who is attracted to both sexes). These feelings may also continue.

Some people disapprove of sexual behavior that is not heterosexual. If you have feelings that are not heterosexual, you may want to be prepared for

Coming Out

$\mathcal{I}$n her book *Understanding Sexual Identity: A Book for Gay and Lesbian Teens and Their Friends,* author Janice Rench encourages kids to feel comfortable with their own sexuality before making any announcements about sexual orientation. She further offers the following list of questions to ask before deciding when or with whom to share that you are gay or lesbian:

• Are you knowledgeable about homosexuality? Family and friends will want to ask you a lot of questions. You need to feel secure about your answers.

• Do you feel comfortable with your sexuality? If you see it as negative, your friends will also be more apt to share that view.

• Has your relationship with your parents been generally good? If you have concerns about their support (financial as well as emotional), you may want to wait to talk about your sexual orientation until you are more independent.

that disapproval. You can get support from people you trust and who will accept your feelings. There are also organizations you can contact.

Guideline #3

Regardless of when and how you experience sexual feelings, there's a major league Big Next Step. It involves guideline #3: Act on your feelings. One key to deciding what you want to do comes from being honest with yourself. Make sure that what you decide to do is not based on "what everybody else is doing" or on ideas you get from media such as movies, magazines, and videos.

Media messages can be very persuasive to both teens and adults. Ever heard the phrase "Sex sells"? It refers to a tactic of including sexy people in ads for products or putting lots of sexy scenes in movies, videos, and books. The sexy people in the ads entice people to buy the products. Sexy scenes in movies, videos, and books entice people to buy tickets to the movies or to buy the videos and books. "Sex sells," right?

The advice [on sex] I got from my friends was not very helpful. . . . It was hard to tell what was "right" for me.

—Fontaine, 18

In recent years, some advertisers have been using younger models than ever in the sexy shots. Sometimes girl models are shown in romantic situations. That's because advertisers are hoping that girls who see the ads will think that they can buy the romance along with the product.

No one is saying that romance is bad or that sex is bad. After all, sex and love lead to pregnancy, which leads to birth. In a very real way, sex is how we all got here! But many adults are concerned that too many young people—particularly girls—believe that sex and romance are the *only* ways to achieve happiness. Some worry that girls too often put others' needs (like what a guy says he wants or peer pressure from classmates) before their own comfort and happiness.

I respect my mom a lot because she taught me to be who I am.

—Carolyn, 14

How does a girl find out what she wants? Discovering that is a complicated process, but it can happen. First, get informed (good old guideline #1). Some of the organizations already mentioned, such as the YWCA, the Girl Scouts, and Girls, Incorporated, have good programs that help girls identify their needs and make good decisions. Planned Parenthood has offices in many cities. This organization offers "peer educator" programs in which teens trained in decision making help other teens.

Girls can also discuss their feelings with someone they trust and respect, like a parent or a school counselor. Talking with an older person may be preferable to talking with friends your own age. "The advice I got from my friends was not very helpful," says Fontaine, 18. Fontaine is a peer educator for Planned Parenthood in Austin, Texas. "They didn't have a lot of basic information right, and we were all so influenced by peer pressure. It was hard to tell what was 'right' for me, and what was just what everybody else was doing."

Check in with You

You can get good information from yourself—if you really listen. That's what Fontaine and other Austin peer educators found. They got clues about what they should do by noticing what activities made them feel good—or bad—about themselves.

"When my boyfriend and I discuss what kind of touching we are both comfortable with before we

My boyfriend and I discuss what kind of touching we are both comfortable with.

—Laurie, 15

do anything, it makes me feel so much better about myself," says Laurie, 15. "And it makes me feel a lot closer to him."

"When I was having a lot of sexual activity with different guys, I started feeling just awful about myself," says Roxana, 20. "I realized that I was doing it for some dumb reasons, like I thought I wasn't pretty enough to have a boyfriend, or I gave him sex because I thought he would like me more."

Some girls even write down a plan for themselves. They describe what kind of romantic and sexual behavior they expect. "A friend of mine has a 'fantasy' plan," notes Alissa, 18. "It spells out what kinds of conditions she wants on a date or in a relationship. If things aren't working out that way, then she knows it's time to go."

It's pretty impossible, of course, to make romance happen the way you'd like. Romance and dating may be down the road a bit for you. Even so, the attitudes you build now can help prepare you to make good decisions later. It's very possible for you to plan

I was [having sex] for dumb reasons, like I thought I wasn't pretty enough to have a boyfriend or . . . I thought he would like me more.

—Roxana, 20

what you want to do with your body. The key is to recognize that pleasures like touching are only good when *you* decide that they're the right thing at the right time.

The same is true for other changes with your body. You can't control when and how these changes happen to you. You can control how you feel about them, though. When you feel okay—or even happy—about them, you'll feel happy about you.

chapter five

Strong Inside and Out

When I did things like rock climbing, I found how hard it is. But once I realized that I can do something I had feared, I began thinking that maybe there are other things I could do.

—*Claire*, 15

Here are a couple of questions for you. Are you very strong? Is your voice very loud?

Hold on before you start thinking about how you can throw a ball really far or how you can holler for a friend so loud that she can hear you two blocks away. First, let's consider what the words "strong" and "voice" *could* mean.

Maybe you know someone who might not seem particularly strong physically. Maybe she's not interested in sports. But she seems to be strong inside. She knows what she wants; she doesn't seem to follow the crowd.

Or perhaps you know someone who's kind of quiet or soft spoken. But when she talks, she speaks with confidence and expressiveness, showing that she likes her unique personality and talents. Experts who study how people express themselves would say that this girl has "found her voice."

Using these definitions, being strong and having a clear voice come from focusing on your inner resources. It's important to try to have a strong and healthy body, of course. But it's hard to have *true* confidence in your outer self—your appearance and physical abilities—without strengthening your inner self. A strong inner self simply means that you listen to what *you* want to say and do, and then *just do it!*

> *I* [was] nervous to try new challenges. I thought if I failed doing them, people would laugh at me.
>
> —Claire, 15

The Old Days

It used to be a lot harder for girls and women to do and say what they wanted. It wasn't that long ago that many girls were discouraged from attending school and were not allowed to play sports.

We Owe
Them

*I*n her book *Voices of Feminism: Past, Present, and Future,* author Joann Bren Guernsey gives us an overview of what women in the 1700s and 1800s faced.

Guernsey highlights the efforts of Mary Wollstonecraft, a British writer whose 1792 work *A Vindication of the Rights of Woman* was among the first to say that men and women should be equal. It became a best-seller.

Abigail Adams, wife of one president and mother to another, sent letter after letter to her husband—who was helping to set up the new U.S. government in the 1700s—demanding political power for women.

Emma Willard pioneered high school education for women, believing they should be exposed to math, science, and other "manly" subjects. We owe women like these a lot for their courage and spirit.

Women were forbidden to vote, and they were barred from many kinds of jobs. They often had no right to own property.

The logic? Females are weak and delicate, went the reasoning. So females can't play sports or do tasks that take strength. Females are supposed to be wives and mothers—why send them to school? Females are not as smart as males—why let them vote or own property? That's (in part) what some people thought for a long time.

Sound ridiculous? Of course it is! But sadly, some of those ideas still linger. There's still an expectation that girls should act "feminine," which seems to be defined as "acting not quite as strong and smart as boys." This expectation may make girls hesitate to speak up in class or stick up for themselves or join in sports and games with boys.

Have you ever decided not to say or do something because you weren't confident enough or because you thought that other people might not approve? If so, that's okay. Chances are that if you're reading this book, you're interested in finding ways to be more confident in body and mind.

You might be inspired by some of the following ideas. They come from girls who are finding ways to redefine what "strong" really means by using their unique bodies and minds.

Take Care of *Your Body*

Keeping your body in good working order just makes sense. A healthy body helps keep your brainpower at its peak. And everybody knows that putting lots of alcohol and drugs in your body doesn't make sense. Girls involved in one Girls, Incorporated program called Friendly PEERsuasion help one another stay away from drugs and alcohol.

Staying away is not a matter of "just saying no." Girls talk about the fact that girls (boys and grown-ups, too) often use drugs and alcohol to help them forget about big-time stresses in their lives—stresses like being ignored or abused by others. Peer pressure can be a very powerful force, too. These girls help one another find solutions for their problems, as well as find healthy ways to replace drugs and alcohol in their lives.

When I participate in sports, I feel like I am part of a team and important for other reasons than my looks.

—Jenny, 11

Challenge *Your Body*

Many girls find that it's fun to play hard at sports, dance, or outside activities. Most girls find their self-confidence increases when they get physically stronger. Several years of karate classes helped Sasha "gain confidence in many ways," as well as "enough physical strength to make sure no one harms me." Jenny, 11, likes sports because "I feel like I am part of a team and important for other reasons than my looks."

The opportunities for girls to participate in sports may be plentiful in many places, but in

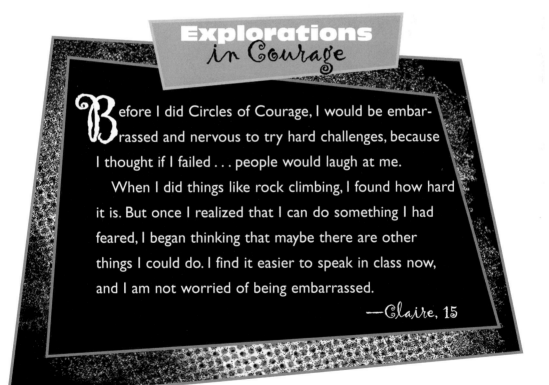

Explorations in Courage

Before I did Circles of Courage, I would be embarrassed and nervous to try hard challenges, because I thought if I failed . . . people would laugh at me.

When I did things like rock climbing, I found how hard it is. But once I realized that I can do something I had feared, I began thinking that maybe there are other things I could do. I find it easier to speak in class now, and I am not worried of being embarrassed.

—Claire, 15

other places, girls find that boys seem to get the best sports options. Girls in Minneapolis, Minnesota, helped begin the Girls' Program to make the city's parks and recreation programs more "girl friendly." The Girls' Program got more coaches and more time for girls' sports. It offers regular get-togethers for girls to do stuff like put on plays and go on field trips.

At the Circles of Courage programs held in the Boston, Massachusetts, area, girls test their bodies and their courage. They go canoeing, rock climbing, and camping by themselves.

Girls in Circles of Courage also do some "exploring" inside themselves. They write in journals and make self-portraits. They talk with one another about how they are courageous in ordinary ways, such as sticking up for others.

And girls don't need to be able-bodied to challenge their bodies. Lots of disabled girls participate in sports, such as wheelchair basketball. Callie, 15, is in a wheelchair with cerebral palsy, and she's also on the cheerleading squad, shouting encouragement and waving pompons.

Defend Yourself

Girls are finding many different ways to respond to hurtful and harmful situations. These can range from insults to date rape (sex that is forced on a girl by her date). At GirlsSpeak, for example, girls learn that self-defense can go beyond any physical moves. This program, held in the Washington, D.C., area, is for girls aged eleven and twelve. It helps girls develop verbal tactics for responding to teasing and rude remarks. It explores ways to "defend" self-confidence when it drops because a girl doesn't feel pretty or thin enough. And yes, girls also learn physical self-defense tactics.

You just can't sit around. We have to do something, such as talking and taking action in a nonviolent way [to counter prejudice in sports].

—Ebony, 12

Girls find out about self-defense through the Empower program in many East Coast schools and clubs. They learn how to be nice to other girls, too. The program's founder, Rosalind Wiseman, believes that many girls can be mean to other girls. Usually when girls act mean, she says, it's because they feel bad about themselves. Girls get tips on how to help build up other girls' confidence instead of tearing it down.

Girls from elementary grades through high school learn how to defend themselves against both physical violence and emotional violence at

Tell Someone

When I was eleven, I had a body that a lot of girls did not have. Many days I would hear painful jokes about my bra straps showing, a maxi pad in my backpack, or just hateful things about how I was developed.

One day I was walking home from my school, and I heard a group of boys talking about me. As I passed, they yelled hateful things and said I was a "b———." I don't deserve to be treated like dirt. Afterward I told my teacher, and they got in detention. Now, two have moved away and one has been clear out of my way.

Even though it doesn't happen anymore, it is still painful. If you have any situations like mine, it is safe to tell someone, or it can lead into emotional and physical violence.

—Adrienne, 13

Brooklyn's Center for Anti-Violence Education in New York. "Now when someone's picking on me, I feel much more confident about what to do," says Theresa, 13.

Girls don't have to take classes, of course, to learn how to stand up for themselves against teasing, insults, and sexual harassment. Sexual harassment happens when someone says or does something to you that is sexually insulting, such as calling you a "whore" or grabbing your breast or snapping your bra strap.

Erica, 13, was harassed by four boys who yelled ugly remarks at her on her way home from school. She tried avoiding them. Then she learned that the same boys were harassing two other girls. So Erica and the other two girls went to their school administrator. The administrator made the boys stop. The boys also wrote an apology to the girls.

Girls should always seek help if they are being sexually abused. Sexual abuse means that someone, usually someone older than you, is making you do sexual activities you don't want to do. No one has the right to abuse you. Some girls who have been abused have been able to make the actions stop on their own. But most often, girls need outside help to make sexual abuse stop. Even girls who've succeeded in stopping abuse on their own recommend getting help from a trusted grown-up or an organization.

Express *Yourself*

You don't have to be supercreative to express yourself. All you have to do is jump into whatever catches your eye—writing, drawing, theater, crafts—and remember that the point is simply to have fun, not to be perfect. Girls who do this often notice that they start feeling confident about who they are and what they do.

Jessica, 14, simply was doing what she loved when she began keeping a diary in second grade. Guess what the diary habit led to? She's written a book on journal writing for girls called *Totally Private and Personal*.

Vanessa, 16, was often depressed by her disability, which has made her deaf and keeps her in a wheelchair. Then she joined the "Living Out Loud Club" in Oakland, California. The club helps girls with physical and learning disabilities build their confidence by making videos and expressing their needs in constructive ways.

Jessica and Vanessa found their "voices." You can find yours, too. Listen. Learn. And then, let it out!

chapter six

𝕭e a **Rebel!**

When your friends treat you like dirt,
the best thing for you to do is not put
up with it.

—*Julie,* 13

o you ever feel like rebelling? When someone
expects you to do something you don't want to do,
do you sometimes feel like just saying "No, I
won't," or "No, I'll do it a different way"?

Good. Once again, we've proved that you're normal. People like parents and teachers sometimes
aren't too happy when kids rebel. Sometimes, that
disapproval happens when preteens and teens
rebel by doing not-too-smart things. (Smoking
cigarettes because it looks "cool" is not a real
smart way to rebel.)

But at other times, a girl might have some very smart and healthy reasons for her choices. Even these choices can sometimes be seen as "rebelling." Remember that part of becoming a grown-up is learning to make decisions that are right for you, even when that's seen as rebelling.

Many of the girls we heard from in this book are rebelling. The things they're rebelling against are just plain bad news for girls. Girls still face gender biases that keep them from being the happy and free-spirited beings they have a right to be. When girls rebel against gender biases, their rebellion is the best thing in the world.

Let's review three of those destructive expectations.

1. Be Thin and Pretty

My true friends make sure I don't get down on myself about looks.

—Brendon, 13

Because of this expectation, girls spend tons of time, tons of money, and tons of tears trying to meet beauty standards that almost everyone admits are unrealistic. Think about what girls could be doing if they spent the same amount of time and effort on other things in their lives! Of course, it's normal to spend some time on appearance. Everybody does that, including boys. But let's be honest. Boys get off easy because they don't wear makeup, and they don't spend that much time on hair. They can certainly choose to buy lots of clothes, but they don't have to be as "body conscious" in them. Because of the generally loose cut of most male clothing, guys don't have to suck in their stomachs and worry about "my big butt" the way girls do in their generally tighter clothes.

Girls are rebelling against the idea that they are only as good as their looks. They're saying "no" (at least sometimes) to advertisers who try to make them feel insecure about their looks so that girls will buy more things. Girls are looking elsewhere—to the normal girls and women around them—for different models of beauty, style, and shape.

2. Changes Are *Embarrassing*

Another expectation we've looked at is that the years when a girl's body changes will be confusing and embarrassing. Too often, girls don't get much support for coping with—and being happy about—the changes that

I used to think that when I got my period, I'd never be able to tell my mom.

— Jessica, 14

happen during the teen years. They're often teased about either being undeveloped or about being too developed. Menstruation—a very important part of changing into a woman—is hardly ever discussed in public. Neither is sexuality. The loudest messages girls get are the "Just say no" messages (like "Just say no to sexual urges") and the "Just say yes" messages (the media especially sends these).

But girls are learning to be okay about their changing bodies, even when others try to shame them. They're even celebrating those changes. They're making decisions about what they'll do with their bodies based on their own needs and wants, not those of others.

My y mom taught me what rights I have and how to get them.

—Carolyn, 14

3. Girls Are Not Assertive

Girls aren't very good at asserting and defending themselves, goes this expectation. Lots of girls admit that they don't know how to defend themselves against harassment and insults. Even when girls are talented at some things, they say they don't often feel self-confident.

That's not a surprise. Many who study how girls

are treated in our culture observe that girls are often still rewarded for being obedient, not assertive. Girls are more often complimented for being pretty than for being talented.

Girls are changing that, too. Girls are learning—both on their own and with the help of people who believe in girls—that they can stand up for themselves and take pride in who they are.

What about you? Are you a rebel? All being a rebel means is that you'll do what you need to do to be all that you can be. Join the rebel ranks—of girls growing up, growing strong.

Resources *for Girls*

If you want to learn more about ways you can be happier
with your body, many programs, organizations, and publications can help. If body issues are making you depressed or
causing you to do harmful things to yourself, try talking to a
parent, an older friend, a school counselor, or a teacher. Or
you could call a crisis hotline—such as 1-800-4-A-CHILD—for
any problem you have, including being abused, using drugs
or alcohol, getting pregnant, or running away from home. The
yellow pages of your telephone book list local resources
under "Crisis Intervention." Phone numbers with an 800 or
an 888 area code are toll free.

Organizations—Mentors and Girl Groups

Volunteers at Big Sisters spend time with and mentor girls.
Some chapters offer a "Life Choices" program that helps girls
make the best decisions for themselves. You can also look in
your phone book for a local Big Brothers Big Sisters number.

> Big Brothers Big Sisters of America
> 230 North 13th Street
> Philadelphia, PA 19107
> (215) 567-7000
> www.bbbsa.org

Girls, Incorporated has many local chapters where girls gather
for fun and learning.

> Girls, Incorporated
> 30 East 33rd Street
> New York, NY 10016
> (212) 689-3700
> www.girlsinc.org

Girl Scouts go way beyond camping these days and offer lots of fun learning experiences. A contemporary issues program helps girls learn about self-esteem, health issues, good relationships, stress management, and other topics. The national office can help you find a local troop.

Girl Scouts of the USA
420 Fifth Avenue
New York, NY 10018-2702
(212) 223-0624
www.gsusa.org

After-school YWCA clubs include PACT, a peer education program in which girls learn to teach other girls about health and sexuality issues, about how to resist peer pressure, and about how to be a leader.

YWCA of the USA
726 Broadway
New York, NY 10003
(800) YWCA-US1
www.ywca.org

Organizations—Self-Esteem and Body Image

The National Association to Advance Fat Acceptance (NAAFA) can help you accept and like the body you have, whether you're overweight or normal-sized but think you're fat. NAAFA offers information and can refer you to local groups.

NAAFA
Post Office Box 188620
Sacramento, CA 95818
(800) 442-1214

The National Eating Disorders Organization (NEDO) offers free information about anorexia, bulimia, and exercise addiction and makes local referrals for treatment.

NEDO
6655 South Yale Avenue
Tulsa, OK 74136
(918) 481-4044
www.laureate.com

Organizations—Sexuality and Body Changes

You can contact the National Gay and Lesbian Task Force (NGLTF) for a referral to a local support group or organization for lesbian, gay, bisexual, and transgender young people.

NGLTF
1700 Kalorama Road, NW
Washington, DC 20009
(202) 332-6483
www.ngltf.org

Planned Parenthood helps with questions about birth control, pregnancy tests, abortion, and sexuality counseling. They can send information. Dialing (800) 230-PLAN automatically connects you with the nearest clinic. Some areas offer a peer education service for girls.

Planned Parenthood Federation of America
810 Seventh Avenue
New York, NY 10019
(800) 829-7732
www.plannedparenthood.org

The Sex Information Education Councils will refer you to local organizations that can help with questions about the body, sex, and pregnancy.

Sex Information Education Councils of the United States
130 West 42nd Street, Suite 350
New York, NY 10036
(212) 819-9770
www.siecus.org

Magazines and Newspapers

Blue Jean, a magazine for older girls, focuses on publishing what young women are "thinking, saying, and doing."

Blue Jean
Post Office Box 507
Victor, NY 14564
(716) 924-4080
www.bluejeanmag.com

New Girl Times is a national newspaper for girls. It has "all the news that's fit to empower," along with fiction, puzzles, and poetry.

New Girl Times
215 West 84th Street
New York, NY 10024
(800) 560-7525

New Moon is a bimonthly magazine that has news and fiction for and about girls, without the usual diet, clothes, and boys articles. *New Moon* is planned by an editorial board of girls aged nine to fourteen and has lots of things written and drawn by girls.

> *New Moon: The Magazine for Girls and Their Dreams*
> Post Office Box 3587
> Duluth, MN 55803
> (800) 381-4743
> www.newmoon.org

Teen Voices is a quarterly magazine written by teen girls about lots of good topics including body image, media stereotyping of girls, racism, sexual abuse, and family relationships. Each issue usually has fiction and poetry, too.

> *Teen Voices*
> Post Office Box 120027
> Boston, MA 02112-0027
> (800) 882-TEEN
> www.teen voices.com

YO!, a quarterly newspaper, is not just for girls, but it has plenty of writing by girls on a wide range of topics important to teens.

> *YO!*
> 450 Mission Street, Suite 204
> San Francisco, CA 94105
> (415) 243-4364

Websites

FeMiNa—at www.femina.com—has a section for girls that includes information on books, careers, games, health, sports, music, technology programs, and links to girls' homepages.

Girl Power—at www.health.org/gpower—has all kinds of sub-categories, including a new one on body image, to go along with information on eating right, staying active, and respecting your body.

GirlTech—at www.girltech.com—encourages girls to explore the world of technology. Subcategories include a bulletin board, tech trips, girl views, cool games, and girls in sports.

Girl Zone—at www.girlzone.com—is governed by a teen advisory board and shares information on books, health, and self-image.

Troom—at www.troom.com—offers information on travel, music, issues, and body changes.

Books

Driscoll, Anne. *Girl to Girl: The Real Deal on Being a Girl Today.* Rockport, MA: Element, 1999.

Girls Know Best: Advice for Girls from Girls on Just About Everything. Hillsboro, OR: Beyond Words, 1997.

Harlan, Judith. *Girl Talk: Staying Strong, Feeling Good, Sticking Together.* New York: Walker, 1997.

Jukes, Mavis. *It's a Girl Thing: How to Stay Healthy, Safe, and in Charge.* New York: Knopf, 1996.

McCoy, Kathy, and Charles Wibbelsman. *The Teenage Body Book.* New York: Putnam, 1999.

Sandler. Sara. *Ophelia Speaks: Adolescent Girls Write about Their Search for Self.* New York: HarperCollins, 1999.

Resources
for Parents and Teachers

Organizations

The catalog of the American Association of University Women (AAUW) lists publications and videos that encourage girls in nontraditional areas and that give advice on handling issues such as sexual harassment. AAUW also sponsors Sister-to-Sister girls' conferences around the country.

AAUW
1111 16th Street NW
Washington, DC 20036-4873
(202) 785-7700
(call (800) 326-AAUW for catalog)
www.aauw.org

Girls, Incorporated provides a variety of resources to teachers and parents to promote girls' self-confidence.

Girls, Incorporated
30 East 33rd Street
New York, NY 10016
(212) 689-3700
www.girlsinc.org

The National Women's History Project has plenty of information and resources about our foremothers. The organization offers a catalog and has a website.

National Women's History Project
7738 Bell Road
Windsor, CA 95492
(707) 838-6000
www.nwhp.org

The Women's College Coalition has a website—called Expect the Best from a Girl—for resources and tips on helping girls get the most out of school and life.

Women's College Coalition
125 Michigan Avenue NE
Washington, DC 20017
(202) 234-0443
www.academic.org

The Women's Educational Equity Act (WEEA) will send a free catalog with plenty of resources to promote girls' self-esteem.

WEEA
Equity Resource Center
EDC 55 Chapel Street
Newton, MA 02458
(800) 225-3088
www.edc.org/womensequity

Books

Bingham, Mindy. *Things Will Be Different for My Daughter: A Practical Guide to Building Her Self-Esteem and Self-Reliance.* New York: Penguin, 1995.

Eagle, Carol. *All That She Can Be: Helping Your Daughter Achieve Her Full Potential and Maintain Her Self-Esteem during the Critical Years of Adolescence.* New York: Simon & Schuster, 1993.

Mann, Judy. *The Difference: Discovering the Ways We Silence Girls.* New York: Warner, 1996.

Odean, Kathleen. *Great Books for Girls: More than 600 Books to Inspire Today's Girls and Tomorrow's Women.* New York: Ballantine, 1997.

Orenstein, Peggy. *SchoolGirls: Young Women, Self-Esteem, and the Confidence Gap.* New York: Bantam Doubleday, 1995.

Pipher, Mary. *Reviving Ophelia: Saving the Selves of Adolescent Girls.* New York: Ballantine, 1995.

Index

About *the Author*

Helen Cordes has had a longtime interest in girls' and
women's issues. The mother of two daughters, she writes for
magazines such as *Parenting, New Moon,* and *The Nation*
and volunteers at a Montessori school. In the past, Cordes
has served as a staff editor at the *Utne Reader* and has
worked as a College Press Service reporter. She lives in
Georgetown, Texas, with her husband, Eric, and their daughters, Jesse and Zoe. *Girl Power in the Mirror* and *Girl Power
in the Classroom* are her first books.